Memorandum on the Musketry Training of the Troops in India 1915-16.

This memorandum is issued by order of the Commander-in-Chief, with the object of reviewing the progress of musketry training during the past year, and indicating directions in which further progress should be sought.

It is to be communicated to all officers concerned.

GEO. M. KIRKPATRICK,

ARMY HEADQUARTERS

SIMLA;

2nd September 1916.

Lieut.-General,
Chief of the General Staff, India.

The Naval & Military Press Ltd

Published by

The Naval & Military Press Ltd
Unit 5 Riverside, Brambleside
Bellbrook Industrial Estate
Uckfield, East Sussex
TN22 1QQ England

Tel: +44 (0)1825 749494

www.naval-military-press.com
www.nmarchive.com

In reprinting in facsimile from the original, any imperfections are inevitably reproduced and the quality may fall short of modern type and cartographic standards.

TABLE OF CONTENTS.

	PAGES.
I. SCHOOLS OF MUSKETRY AND VARIOUS COURSES OF INSTRUCTION.	

PARAS.
1. PROGRESS OF INSTRUCTION AT THE SCHOOLS 1
2. Preparation of candidates for courses 2
3. Senior officers courses 3

II. ANNUAL COURSE.
4. Classification 4
5. Ditto 5
6. Cavalry 6
7. British Infantry Depôts 7
8. Garrison Battalions 8
9. Indian Depôts 8
10. Volunteers 10
11. Night Firing 10
12. Fire Direction and Control 11
13. Field Practices 12

III. GENERAL.
14. Judging Distance and Visual Training 14
15. Handling of Arms 14
16. Machine Guns 14
17. Ammunition, ·22 Bore 16
18. Care of Arms 16
19. Returns 16
20. 17

MEMORANDUM ON THE MUSKETRY TRAINING OF THE TROOPS IN INDIA 1915-16.

SCHOOLS OF MUSKETRY AND VARIOUS COURSES OF INSTRUCTION.

I. PROGRESS OF INSTRUCTION AT THE SCHOOLS.

1. Musketry and Machine Gun Courses have been held at the schools at Pachmarhi, Changla Gali and Satara, and the following officers and non-commissioned officers of the British and Indian services qualified during the year.

Musketry.

British Service regular officers	39
Indian Army regular officers	75
Territorial officers	201
British non-commissioned officers (regulars)	72
British non-commissioned officers (territorials)	221
Indian officers	40
Indian non-commissioned officers	185

Machine Gun.

British Service regular officers	...	55
Indian Army regular officers	...	97
Territorial force officers ...	...	89
British non-commissioned officers (regulars)	...	71
British non-commissioned officers (territorials)	...	60
Indian officers ...	...	8
Indian non-commissioned officers	...	113

In addition to the above, a special musketry and machine gun course, for 50 young officers of under 12 months' service, was held at Changla Gali from April to June.

These officers were not considered to have qualified in musketry and machine gun, as it was considered undesirable that such young officers should be debarred from attending courses later in their service.

2. The standard of preparation of students attending the schools varied considerably—as was to be expected under the abnormal conditions prevailing during the year. In many cases only very short notice could be given to students detailed to attend courses.

No entrance examination has been held since the war began, as it was considered better, in the interests of the army, to make the best of the material available, rather than to create vacancies at the schools by sending any students away. For similar reasons all examinations have been marked with rather more leniency than at ordinary times.

3. Five senior officers' classes have been held in divisions, and officers of the following arms attended.—

General officers	2
Staff	4
British cavalry	3
Indian cavalry	6
Royal artillery	2
Royal engineers	1
British infantry	3
Indian infantry	5
Territorial infantry	101
Volunteers	1

The courses were attended by officers from all divisions in India and Burma, and included 26 commanding officers.

II. Annual Course.

4. Classification. *Regulars.*—The averages of aggregates obtained by the several arms in the classification practices of the annual course are as follows:—

	1913-14.	1914-15.	1915-16.
British cavalry	116·16	114·63	119·93
British artillery	94·89	89·05	92·55
British infantry	110·11	111·89	113·58
Territorial infantry	...	85·76	92·75
Indian cavalry	79·74	80·18	79·59
Indian cavalry, depôts		...	76·31
Indian artillery	85·55	90·39	89·46
Sappers and miners	81·76	76·68	77·95
Indian infantry	82·67	83·30	82·11
Indian infantry, depôts	...	...	72·40

5. These results may be considered generally satisfactory. British regular troops, in each case, show an improvement on the previous year—owing probably to the large number of old soldiers in the ranks.

The average made by the Territorial units is also a great advance on the previous year, though a good many of the battalions reported on were firing their first course in India, and in these a large number of men were firing the first course of their service. The number of indifferent shots is still unduly large. Of 16,690 men classified there are 7,186 (43 per cent.) 2nd class, and 3,448 (20 per cent.) 3rd class shots. These numbers and the large number of men in nearly every battalion who failed to qualify in Part I, Table B, at the first attempt, show the need for every effort being made to improve the elementary training.

It is satisfactory to note the improvement made by battalions firing their second course in India. Among the 11 battalions now reported on for the second time, the average has risen from 82·9 to 99·3.

The special efforts made to raise the standard of elementary instruction—the training of large numbers of officers and non-commissioned officers at the schools, the holding of senior officer courses, which were attended by nearly every Territorial commanding officer, and the visits paid to units by members of the musketry staff—may be expected to produce a further marked improvement this year.

The averages made by Indian cavalry and infantry units are satisfactory—though training was often carried out under considerable difficulties,'and there is a demand for more trained instructors.

The average shown for Indian infantry depôts was made by the comparatively small numbers who fired Table B. The figure is unsatisfactory and shows the urgent need for more trained instructors and closer attention being paid to the elementary training at these depôts.

6. *Cavalry.*—The experience of the war seems to prove conclusively that the ability to use the rifle effectively is almost as important for cavalry as for infantry. This is not only so as regards fighting in France, where cavalry have had few opportunities so far of mounted action and where units have been employed in the trenches from time to time, but also in Mesopotamia, where dismounted action has often played an important part. In this fighting the efficiency of units has varied greatly in accordance with the thoroughness of their previous musketry training.

In the British cavalry regiments in India the training for the past year has been carried out on sound lines.

The musketry training of the 17 Indian cavalry regiments in India has varied greatly. Two regiments fired special courses. Of the remainder the numbers exercised at collective field practices were about half of those exercised at range practices. In several regiments no collective practices were carried out. Of 12 regiments who fired these practices only 4 appear to have fired any troop practices. Unless the troop, the normal fire unit, has been brought to an adequate standard of efficiency, only possible at troop practices, squadron practices are likely to be a mere waste of ammunition.

In only 5 regiments were fire direction practices correctly carried out.

Most regiments have to spend much time on the training of remounts at present. Time should, however, be found for the more essential items of musketry training. It is possible that the training of remounts might, in its later stages, be usefully combined with the training of men in fire action.

7. *British Infantry Depôts*—The numbers trained are small, the results being generally satisfactory.

8. *Garrison Battalions.*—None of these battalions have yet fired classification practices.

Pending their re-armament with short M. L. E. rifles, they have been ordered to fire Table A and parts IV, V, and. VI and fire direction practices of Table B only.

Every endeavour should be made to select capable and intelligent non-commissioned officers to attend the schools during the current year.

9. *Indian Depôts.*—The musketry training carried out at Indian depôts was very unequal. The standard of training at some depôts is very low, and important items are often omitted.

In many cases far more attention is required to instruction in fire control and discipline.

It is recognised that the musketry training at depôts is carried out under considerable difficulties, owing to shortness of time and rifles and the want of trained instructors, but every endeavour must be made to raise the standard of training.

Shorter courses have recently been introduced at the schools, and it is hoped that this will enable a large number of British officers and Indian ranks from depôts to attend courses without unduly disturbing the depôt work.

If a man is unable to handle his rifle correctly and shoot reasonably well he is of little use in the firing line. If he has not been grounded in fire control and discipline he is likely to be a source of danger, as wild firing, and firing without orders by a few men, is likely to lead to loss of control by commanders.

It is essential that close attention should be paid by local staffs to the musketry training carried on at depôts. A perusal of the returns indicates that the importance of this training is not always realised. In some cases the only criticism is a comment on the number of 3rd class shots.

The instructions contained in the Chief of the General Staff's No. 10152-3, dated 3rd April 1916, and 10152-4, dated 27th April 1916, should be closely followed.

10. *Volunteers.*—Percentages of marksmen, 1st and 2nd class shots are as follows:—

Year.	Marksmen.	1st Class.	2nd Class.	3rd Class.
1913-14	21·17	36·58	40·96	1·28
1914-15	20·69	36·06	42·51	0·72
1915-16	22·48	38·37	38·41	0·71

The results of the range practices are satisfactory, the numbers exercised being approximately the same as in the previous year.

In comparatively few units have any individual or collective field practices been carried out. On the other hand nearly every unit has carried out battalion field firing.

The all round efficiency of Volunteer units would be greatly increased if a series of individual and collective field practices were carried out, special attention being paid to section practices. If ammunition runs short battalion field firing might be omitted without detriment to efficiency.

11. *Night Firing.*—No mention of this is made in the returns. Men should be taught with dummy cartridges to handle their rifles in the dark, both in the

open and in trenches. A few night firing practices should be carried out.

12. *Fire Direction and Control.*—Too little attention is paid to this most important item of training.

Officers and non-commissioned officers attending the schools are constantly found to possess little or no knowledge of how to direct or control the fire of a unit.

Its importance can hardly be over-rated. Unless it has been carefully studied, taught, and practised in peace training, fire in the field must of necessity be uncontrolled and largely ineffective.

Good fire direction and control is equally necessary both in regular warfare and Indian frontier operations where fire may often have to be delivered against an invisible enemy, or against unoccupied positions in order to deny these to the enemy.

There is a tendency to think that it is difficult to find time and opportunity for this training. There would be no such feeling if it were more generally realised how much valuable instruction and practice can be given in short periods of time, close to barracks, whenever a few non-commissioned officers and men happen to be available.

Landscape targets might be more freely used with

advantage, and more use should be made of blank ammunition.

Many methods of carrying out this training are thoroughly taught at the schools and it should be insisted upon that due attention is paid to the matter in units.

13. *Field Practices.*—Large numbers of men were exercised at field practices during the year.

(i) Among the Indian infantry units now in India 24,985 men were fully exercised in the range practices, while the average numbers firing Part IV (Individual field practices) were 16,083 only, and those firing Part VI (Collective field practices) only 11,613.

Part V (Fire direction practices) was often omitted.

Musketry training was doubtless much interfered with during the year, but it would appear that more opportunities might have been taken to fire these practices.

(ii) Among territorial battalions, while 16,690 men were exercised in range practices, only 8,007 fired Part IV, and 7,102 Part VI. Part V was omitted or wrongly carried out in 16 battalions.

In the individual field practices the necessity for giving individual instruction in working under practical conditions is often overlooked. Tactical schemes are out of place in these practices. There must be a target for each firer and the result of each shot must be made known; and there must be close criticism of each individual to ensure the points mentioned in paragraph 508, Musketry Regulations, Part I, being driven home. These practices should include some to be fired from a standing trench, instruction in this having been previously given with dummy cartridges. The ability to fire quickly and accurately at short range should be developed. Many useful practices can be carried out on a classification range where other ground is not available.

Very few section practices were carried out in most units. Special attention should be given to the contents of Chief of General Staff's No. 13289-1, dated 15th January 1916.

The importance of the practices for the smaller fire units cannot be too often emphasised. Success in the field, under modern conditions, depends very largely on the efficiency of the small units. It is in these practices that commanders and men have a chance of learning to work together under practical conditions.

Anything in the nature of a set piece, or the introduction of elaborate schemes should be avoided.

The simpler the conditions under which a practice is carried out, the more instructive it is likely to be. Paragraph 548, Musketry Regulations, Part I, contains valuable instructions which are frequently overlooked.

III. GENERAL.

14. *Judging distance and visual training.*—More attention is required to this important subject. The quarterly judging distance tests must be regularly carried out and it must be remembered that these tests are of no value unless carried out under practical service conditions.

15. *Handling of Arms.*—Attention is directed to India Army Order 566 of 1916. All men should be frequently exercised in handling the rifles with the " cut-off " open.

16. *Machine guns.*—It is evident that much more attention has been paid to machine gun training than in previous years. There is, however, some danger of training running on wrong lines. While it is desirable to have as many men as possible trained as machine gunners, over and above those forming the two service sections, this may easily be carried too far. It is liable to cause the service sections to be deprived of the guns for training purposes for a considerable time, to the detriment of their all round efficiency.

www.ingramcontent.com/pod-product-compliance
Lightning Source LLC
Chambersburg PA
CBHW070051070426
42449CB00012BA/3237